PREVENTIVE MAINTENANCE

Ricky Smith CMRP, CRL
Doug Stangier CMRP, CRL

Preventive maintenance is misunderstood by many maintenance reliability professionals. This book was developed to establish just how simple it can be.

PREVENTIVE MAINTENANCE
MADE SIMPLE

Ricky Smith CMRP, CRL
Doug Stangier CMRP, CRL

ISBN 978-1-941872-43-7
HF112016

©2016 Reliabilityweb.com
Printed in the United States of America.
All rights reserved.

This book, or any parts thereof, may not be reproduced, stored in a retrieval system, or transmitted in any form without the permission of the Publisher.

Opinions expressed in this book are solely the authors' and do not necessarily reflect the views of the Publisher.

Publisher: Terrence O'Hanlon
Design and Layout: Jocelyn Brown

For information: Reliabilityweb.com
www.reliabilityweb.com
8991 Daniels Center Drive, Suite 105, Ft. Myers, FL 33912
Toll Free: 888-575-1245 | Phone: 239-333-2500
E-mail: customerservice@reliabilityweb.com

10 9 8 7 6 5 4 3 2 1

Contents

Introduction v

Chapter 1
What Is Preventive Maintenance? 1

Chapter 2
The 10% Rule of Preventive Maintenance 7

Chapter 3
What Is Reliability Based Preventive Maintenance? 11

Chapter 4
Enhanced Sensory PM Inspections 27

Chapter 5
Writing Effective Work Procedures 37

Chapter 6
Five Tips for Optimizing a PM Program 43

Chapter 7
Preventive Maintenance Metrics 53

About the Authors 57

INTRODUCTION

Optimizing a PM Program–Keeping It Simple

How many times have we heard that "we need to simplify or optimize our PM programs?" I know I have heard this statement a number of times over the past several years and then heard the struggles people have had in doing so successfully.

I have looked for a simple, yet effective method to perform this task that wouldn't compromise the integrity of the program and have yet to find one. Recently, while I was attending a maintenance reliability conference, I ran into Ricky Smith and we got talking about the topic and realized we both shared a passion for the subject and a similar frustration for the lack of a simple, yet effective optimization process. That is when we decided to do something about it ourselves.

First of all, people need to understand what the purpose and basic fundamentals of a PM program are before they can tackle the optimization part. The very first thing to do is to ensure you have at least a basic PM program and if you don't, you are in the wrong line of work. The second thing is to make sure that, at a minimum, your critical assets are covered by some type of PM, even if it's relying on the old "eyeometer," "handometer" and "earometer" to ensure you are at least checking your equipment.

The reasons for performing PMs are to add value to your workload and be able to detect failures early enough to be able to plan and schedule the repairs as needed. If done properly, your assets will run reliably and ultimately contribute to the bottom line, which is the end goal. That said, it becomes very easy for companies to do what is called "knee-jerk" PMs whenever they experience a failure and end up flooding their workforce with hours of non-value adding work and frustrating their employees. This scenario is as bad as not having a PM program, as most of the time you end up not inspecting the right things, the right way, or at the right time. The frequency of your inspections is also critical, as in, if you don't inspect your equipment often enough, it may be too late to detect a failure, or inspect too often and find no errors, or worse yet, risk introducing failures, but we will cover that a little later.

So, because the title of this book is "Preventive Maintenance – Made Simple," we are going to assume (hope) you already have at least a very basic PM program in place. Now, we will lay out the process which will enable you to gain value from your program, as well as credibility from your team and your employer.

So, let's get started as Ricky and I share our thoughts on the process and lead you through another "Made Simple" exercise, one which will have a profound impact on your organization.

–Doug Stangier

CHAPTER

What Is Preventive Maintenance?

Preventive Maintenance (PM) is a maintenance strategy that, if applied effectively, can extend the life of the equipment through inspection, lubrication and inspections for a specific failure mode early enough for the part or component to be changed before a failure occurs. It also includes methods to prevent a failure mode from occurring, such as lubrication, which must be conducted in a controlled experiment.

A PM program is developed using a guided logic approach and is task oriented, rather than maintenance process oriented. This eliminates the confusion associated with the various interpretations across different industries of terms such as condition monitoring, on condition, hard time, etc. By using a task oriented concept, it is possible to see the whole maintenance program reflected for a given item. A decision logic tree is used to identify applicable maintenance tasks. Servicing and lubrication are included as part of the logic diagram as this ensures an important task category is considered each time an item is analyzed.

Maintenance Program Content

The content of the maintenance program itself consists of two groups of tasks.

1. **A group of preventive maintenance tasks, which include failure-finding tasks, scheduled to be accomplished at specified intervals or based on condition.**

    ▶ The objective of these tasks is to identify and prevent deterioration below inherent safety and reliability levels.

- It is this group of tasks, that is determined by reliability centered maintenance (RCM) analysis. The program contains tasks, such as lubrication PMs, visual inspections, filter cleaning, replacing PMs, and so on based on time and operating condition.

2. A group of nonscheduled maintenance tasks that result from:

    - Findings from the scheduled tasks accomplished at specified intervals of time or usage.
    - Reports of malfunctions or indications of impending failure, including automated detection.
    - The objective of this second group of tasks to maintain or restore the equipment to an acceptable condition to which it can perform its required function.

An effective program is one that schedules only those tasks necessary to meet the stated objectives. It does not schedule additional tasks that will increase maintenance costs without a corresponding increase in protection of the inherent level of reliability. Experience has clearly demonstrated that reliability decreases when inappropriate or unnecessary maintenance tasks are performed. This is due to increased incidents of maintainer-induced faults.

Preventive maintenance, in the most basic terms, is:

Lubrication/servicing

Operational/visual/ automated checks

Inspection/functional test/ condition monitoring

Restoration

Discard

Sometimes, preventive maintenance just doesn't work. That's when it's time to stop the collective insanity and start learning from others.

For many years, maintenance and operations professionals performed and managed preventive maintenance on every type of equipment, never asking themselves why the equipment continued to fail even after PM had just been conducted. It was not uncommon for maintenance supervisors to always have high compliance rates and a high number of recurring equipment breakdowns.

It makes you wonder how it is possible that a maintenance professional could perform preventive maintenance on equipment that continues to fail?

One will know now when a PM program is flawed because it is essentially a reactive maintenance program that relies mainly on time-based PM tasks. These tasks follow manufacturers' suggestions and knowledge one has learned through one's maintenance experience. Having no technical justification for any task other than, "we always do it this way," or "it's the latest predictive technology" so "we can't stop doing it now or we'll risk more failures," is the definition of insanity

Research that changed the way maintenance reliability professionals think about failures and PM actually started more than forty years ago, yet many plants and facilities are still falling apart today. It's time to stop the collective insanity. If you face the same problems on a daily basis, sometimes with little hope in sight, the following chapters provide a solution if you have the discipline to execute PM in a control state and measure the results based on good metrics.

Research on equipment failures during the past thirty or so years has proven that more than eighty percent of failures aren't related to equipment age or use. The implication of the finding is that less than twenty percent of proactive maintenance tasks should be driven by time, equipment age, or usage. The majority (i.e., more than eighty percent) should be predictive and detective forms of proactive maintenance. Predictive maintenance (PdM) is the use of technology or some form of condition monitoring to predict equipment failure. Detective maintenance refers to work that determines whether a failure has already occurred. It applies well to hidden failures that aren't, at least initially, evident when they occur.

With this new understanding of failures, you can migrate your department from operating in reactive mode to operating in proactive mode. The key dif-

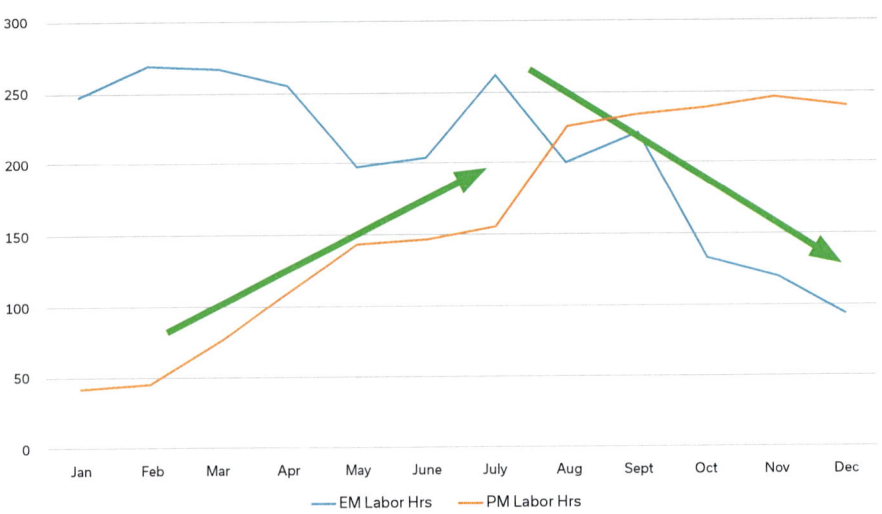

Figure 1.1: Preventive hours vs. emergency work hours

ference is that programs will be focused now on monitoring asset health and letting that determine the maintenance work to be performed proactively.

The research further shows that once you truly understand an asset's failure modes or causes, your program will look more like best in class. It will be an example of a maintenance program that transformed from reactive maintenance to a proactive maintenance program.

Focusing on early detection or identification of specific failure modes can reduce equipment failures by thirty to fifty percent and more. The business impact of a well-defined proactive maintenance program is huge. You'll increase equipment reliability, reduce capital replacement costs, achieve higher equipment availability and reduce maintenance costs. The soft benefits are a motivated workforce, a less stressed management team, more time at home, etc.

While the numbers will get management to support a project to prove the benefits on just one asset, once they see the size of the opportunity and the soft benefits, the next question will be, "What is your plan to roll this out on the rest of our critical assets?" Allow management to work with you to develop the plan. They'll feel some ownership of the process.

After running a compliant PM program for years, you will find you cannot rely on time-based maintenance alone because most failures are random. Research and experience in applying that research has proven that there's a better way to run the business of maintenance. The properly balanced use of predictive, detective and time-based maintenance forms a successful proactive maintenance program.

With such a huge potential to improve business competitiveness, maintenance managers have a great vehicle for generating interest and support among senior management, all of whom are looking for a rapid return.

CHAPTER 2

The 10% Rule of Preventive Maintenance

Many organizations use the PM compliance metric as a measurement of their maintenance department's performance. This metric is often viewed by professionals as a joke because if your PM compliance is high but you continue to have many reliability issues, then the metric has no meaning. There have been organizations with one hundred percent PM compliance, but over ten percent downtime due to reliability issues. Of course, many different issues could contribute to this problem.

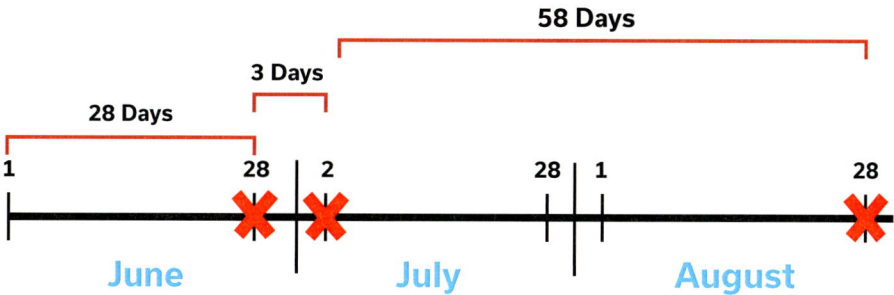

- **30-day PM** - Must be completed within three days or PM is "Out of Compliance"
- **"Out of Compliance"** means more equipment failures and higher maintenance costs because of variation in execution

Figure 2.1: A simple rule: you cannot perform preventive maintenance that continues to break down; something is wrong.

Chapter 2

However, there is a solution to the PM compliance metric to make it believable and truly help you feel confident that it is a true measurement of compliance to your PM program. This solution, which has been tested and proven, requires you to manage your PM program as a controlled experiment. By doing so, you can control reliability with more reliable accuracy.

Now, in order to have a controlled experiment, you must control the variables, such as time. Most PMs are time based, therefore, controlling the variance in your PM schedule would allow you to control reliability better and help you make better decisions.

The 10% rule of preventive maintenance simply states that:

A time-based PM must be accomplished in ten percent of the time frequency or it is out of compliance.

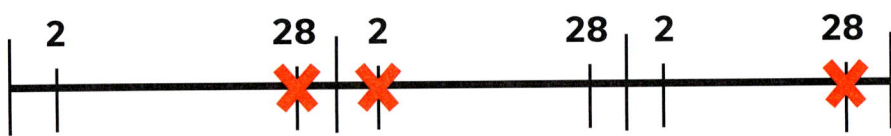

Figure 2.2: This figure illustrates how many organizations perform a monthly (30-day) preventive maintenance strategy applied to a specific component.

1. At the beginning of the first month, a maintenance manager notices a production line is having problems, but tells the maintenance supervisor to put off the PMs until the end of the month.

2. At the end of the month, the maintenance manager tells the maintenance supervisor to make sure all PMs are completed so they meet one hundred percent PM compliance.

3. At the beginning of the next month, the maintenance manager sees the equipment running well and tells the maintenance supervisor to complete the PM now because at the end of the month, the equipment will probably be running badly as usual and with the PMs completed early, they meet their PM compliance.

4. At the beginning of the next month, the equipment is running badly, as expected, so the maintenance manager tells the maintenance supervisor to put off the PM to the end of the month because they do not have time to complete it at this time.

If an organization applies the ten percent rule of PM, then the most critical PMs will be conducted within ten percent of the time frequency. For example, if the PM is conducted outside of three days from the due date, it is out of compliance. What this does is it allows the equipment to be maintained in a controlled state and reduces variation in equipment reliability.

PM is a controlled experiment because it is performed on an asset within a specific time frequency and with a repeatable and measurable PM procedure.

Recommendation: Focus the 10% rule on the time-based PMs you are performing on your critical assets first. These critical assets are the ones that will get you in trouble if their reliability is low. Measure their PM compliance separately from the rest of the equipment. In addition, measure equipment capacity on these assets in order to see the effect of the 10% rule.

One company went from one hundred percent PM compliance to fifty percent overnight because it decided to measure PM compliance using the 10% rule on all assets, but equipment uptime went from eighty-nine percent to ninety-four percent in as little as three months as a result of following this process.

You probably have been taught by everyone that one hundred percent is the best, but the number is whatever the number may be as long as capacity or uptime continues to rise.

The 10% rule is basically a guideline, which if followed, makes you complete your PMs on time as planned.

CHAPTER

What Is Reliability Based Preventive Maintenance?

This chapter describes the tasks in the development of a reliability based preventive maintenance program for both new and in-service equipment. In the development of a program, the principal tools, illustrated in Figure 3.2, are the progressive logic diagram and task selection criteria. Progressive logic is the basis of an evaluation technique applied to each **functionally significant item (FSI)** using the technical data available. Principally, the evaluations are based on the items' functional failures and failure causes. The development of a reliability based preventive maintenance program is based on the following:

- Identification of functionally significant items (FSIs);
- Identification of applicable and effective preventive maintenance tasks using the decision tree logic.

A functionally significant item is an item whose failure would affect safety or could have significant operational or economic impact in a particular operating or maintenance context.

Figure 3.1: Alignment PM inspection

The identification process of FSIs is based on the anticipated consequences of failures using an analytical approach and good engineering judgment. FSIs also use a top-down approach and are conducted first at the system level, then at the subsystem level and, where appropriate, down to the component level. An iterative process should be followed in identifying FSIs. Systems and subsystem boundaries and functions are first identified. This permits selection of critical systems for further analysis, which involves a more comprehensive and detailed definition of the system, system functions and system functional failures.

The procedures below show a comprehensive set of tasks in the FSI Identification Process. All these tasks should be applied for complex or new equipment. However, in the case of well-established or simple equipment where functions and functional degradation/failures are well recognized, tasks listed under the "system analysis" heading can be covered very quickly. They should, however, be documented to confirm they were considered. The depth and rigor used in the application of these tasks will also vary with the complexity and newness of the equipment.

Information Collection

Equipment information provides the basis for the evaluation and should be assembled prior to the start of the analysis and supplemented as the need arises. The following should be included:

- ▶ Requirements for equipment and its associated systems, including regulatory requirements;
- ▶ Design and maintenance documentation;
- ▶ Performance feedback, including maintenance and failure data.

Also, in order to guarantee completeness and avoid duplication, the evaluation should be based on an appropriate and logical breakdown of the equipment.

System Analysis

The tasks described in the information collection step define the procedure for the identification of the functionally significant items and the subsequent

What Is Reliability Based Preventive Maintenance?

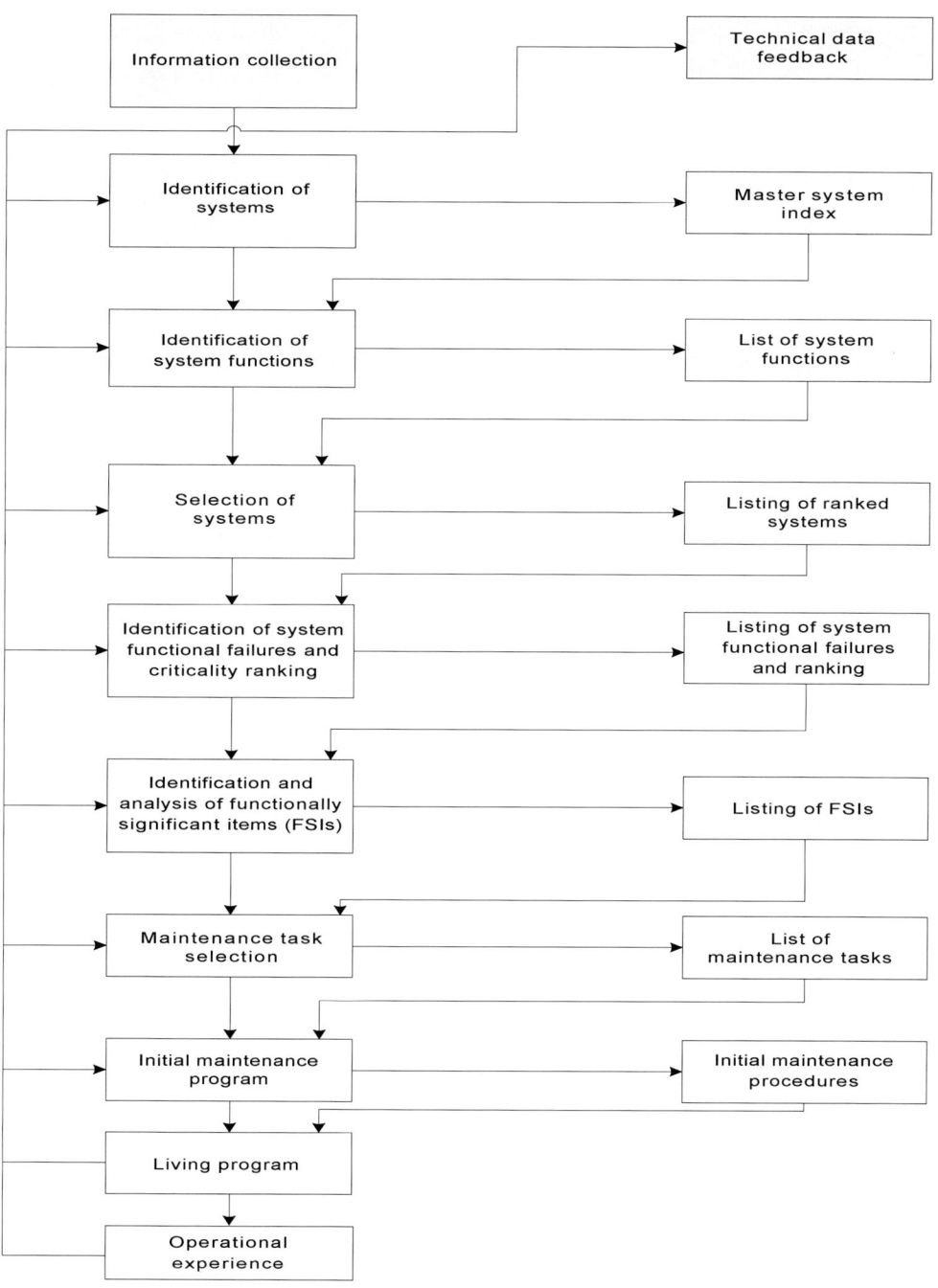

Figure 3.2: Development tasks of a reliability based preventive maintenance program

maintenance task selection and implementation. It should be noted that tasks can be tailored to meet the requirements of particular industries and the emphasis placed on each task will depend on the nature of that industry.

Identification of Systems

The objective of this task is to partition the equipment into systems, grouping the components contributing to the achievement of well identified functions and identifying the system's boundaries. Sometimes, it is necessary to perform further partitioning into the subsystems that perform functions critical to system performance. The system's boundaries may not be limited by the physical boundaries of the systems, which may overlap.

Frequently, the equipment is already partitioned into systems through industry specific partitioning schemes. This partitioning should be reviewed and adjusted where necessary to ensure it is functionally oriented. The results of equipment partitioning should be documented in a master system index that identifies systems, components and boundaries.

Identification of System Functions

The objective of this task is to determine the main and auxiliary functions performed by the systems and subsystems. The use of functional block diagrams will assist in the identification of system functions. The function definition describes the actions or requirements the system or subsystem should accomplish, sometimes in terms of performance capabilities within the specified limits. The functions should be identified for all modes of equipment operation.

Reviewing design specifications, design descriptions and operating procedures, including safety, abnormal operations and emergency instructions, may determine the main and auxiliary functions. Functions, such as testing or preparations for maintenance, may be omitted if not considered important. However, the reasons for omissions must be given. The product of this task is a listing of system functions.

Selection of Systems

The objective of this task is to select and prioritize systems that will be included in the RCM program because of their significance to equipment safety, availability, or economics. The methods used to select and prioritize the systems can be divided into:

- Qualitative methods based on past history and collective engineering judgment.
- Quantitative methods based on quantitative criteria, such as criticality rating, safety factors, probability of failure, failure rate, lifecycle cost, etc., used to evaluate the importance of system degradation and/or failure on equipment safety, performance and costs. Implementation of this approach is facilitated when appropriate models and data banks exist.
- A combination of qualitative and quantitative methods.

The product of this task is a listing of systems ranked by criticality. The systems, together with the methods, criteria used and the results, should be documented.

Identification of System Functional Failures and Criticality Ranking

The objective of this task is to identify system functional degradation/failures and prioritize them. The functional degradation/failures of a system for each function should be identified, ranked by criticality and documented.

Since each system's functional failure may have different impacts on safety, availability, or maintenance cost, it is necessary to rank and prioritize each one. The ranking takes into account probability of occurrence and consequences of failure. Qualitative methods based on collective engineering judgment and the analysis of operating experience can be used. Quantitative methods of simplified failure mode and effects analysis (SFMEA) or risk analysis also can be used.

The ranking represents one of the most important tasks in RCM analysis. Too conservative a ranking may lead to an excessive preventive maintenance program. Conversely, a lower ranking may result in excessive failures and a potential safety impact. In both cases, a non-optimized maintenance program will result. The outputs of this task are:

- Listing of system functional degradation/failures and their characteristics;
- Ranking list of system functional degradation/failures.

Chapter 3

Identification and Analysis of Functionally Significant Items (FSIs)

Based on the identification of system functions, functional degradation/failures and effects, and collective engineering judgment, it is possible to identify and develop a list of FSIs candidates. As noted before, these are items whose failures could affect safety, be undetectable during normal operation, and have significant operational and economic impact. The output of this task is a list of FSIs candidates.

Once an FSI list has been developed, a method such as failure mode and effects analysis (FMEA) should be used to identify information that is necessary for the logic tree evaluation of each FSI. These examples refer to the failure of a pump providing cooling water flow:

- ▶ **Function:** The normal characteristic actions of the item (e.g., to provide cooling water flow at 100 l/s to 240 l/s to the heat exchanger);
- ▶ **Functional failure:** How the item fails to perform its function (e.g., pump fails to provide required flow);
- ▶ **Failure cause:** Why the functional failure occurs (e.g., bearing failure);
- ▶ **Failure effect:** What the immediate effect and the wider consequence of each functional failure is (e.g., inadequate cooling leading to overheating and failure of the system).

The FSI failure analysis is intended to identify functional failures and failure causes. Failures not considered as credible, such as those resulting solely from undetected manufacturing faults, unlikely failure mechanisms, or unlikely external occurrences, should be recorded as having been considered and the factors that caused them assessed as not credible and stated.

Prior to applying the decision logic tree analysis to each FSI, preliminary worksheets need to be completed that clearly define the FSI, its functions, functional failures, failure causes, failure effects and any additional data pertinent to the item (e.g., manufacturer's part number, a brief description of the item, predicted or measured failure rate, hidden functions, redundancy, etc.). These worksheets should be designed to meet the user's requirements.

From this analysis, the critical FSIs can be identified, including those that have both significant functional effects and a high probability of failure; a me-

What Is Reliability Based Preventive Maintenance?

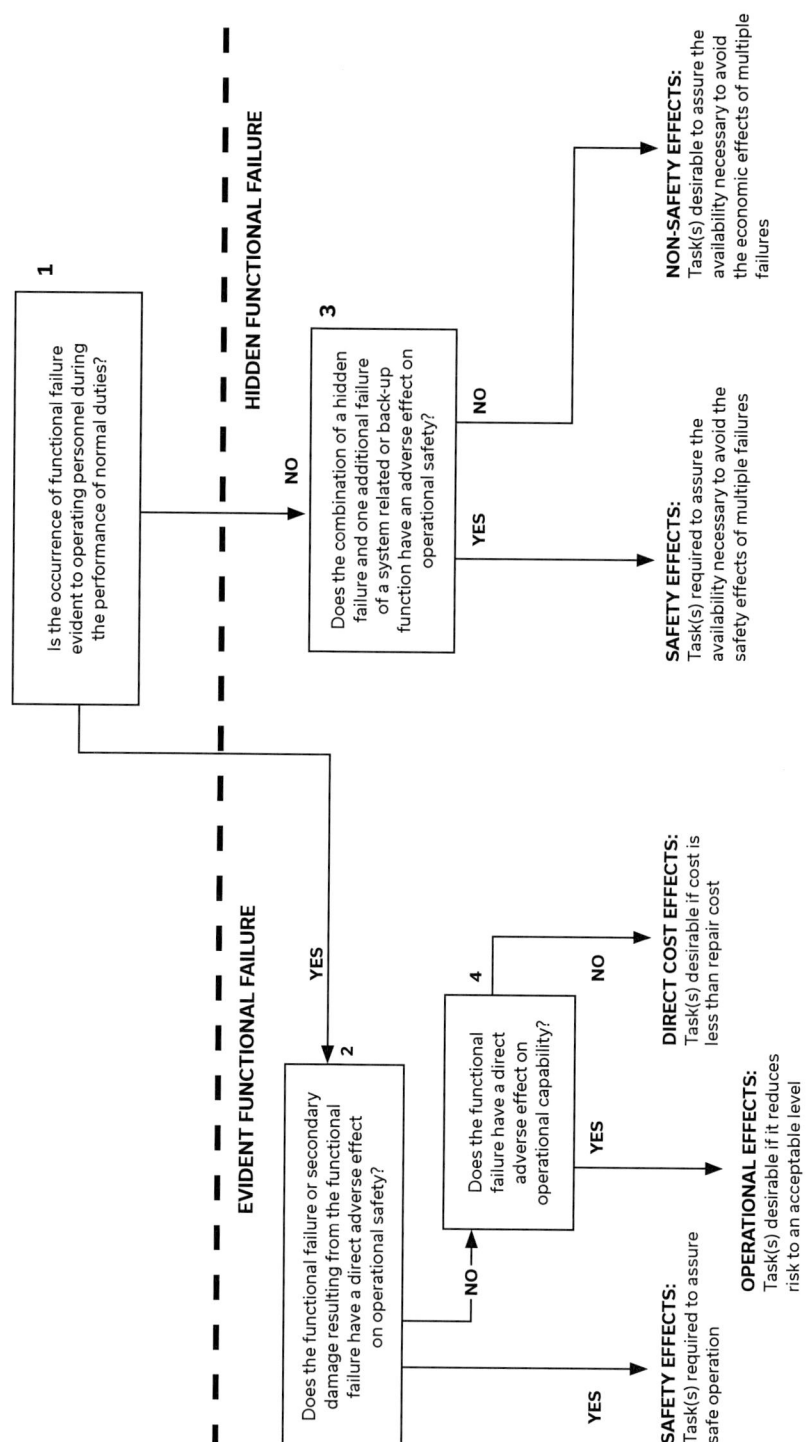

Figure 3.3: Decision logic tree

dium probability of failure, but judged critical; or a significantly poor maintenance record.

Maintenance Task Selection (Decision Logic Tree Analysis)

The approach used for identifying applicable and effective preventive maintenance tasks is one that provides a logic path for addressing each FSI functional failure. The decision logic tree (Figure 3.3) uses a group of sequential YES/NO questions to classify or characterize each functional failure. The answers to the YES/NO questions determine the direction of the analysis flow and help determine the consequences of the FSI functional failure, which may be different for each failure cause. Further progression of the analysis will ascertain if there is an applicable and effective maintenance task that will prevent or mitigate it. The resultant tasks and related intervals will form the initial scheduled maintenance program.

NOTE: Proceeding with the logic tree analysis with inadequate or incomplete FSI failure information could lead to safety critical failures due to inappropriate, omitted, or unnecessary maintenance, increased costs due to unnecessary scheduled maintenance activity, or both.

Levels of Analysis

Two levels are apparent in the decision logic.

- ▶ The first level (Questions 1, 2, 3 and 4) in Figure 3.4 requires an evaluation of each functional degradation/failure for determination of the ultimate effect category (e.g., evident safety, evident operational, evident direct cost, hidden safety, hidden non-safety, or none).
- ▶ The second level in Figure 3.5 takes the failure causes for each functional degradation/failure into account in order to select the specific type of tasks.

First Level Analysis (Determination of Effects)

Consequence of failure, which could include degradation, is evaluated at the first level using four basic questions indicated in Figure 3.4.

NOTE: The analysis should not proceed through the first level unless there is a full and complete understanding of the particular functional failure.

What Is Reliability Based Preventive Maintenance?

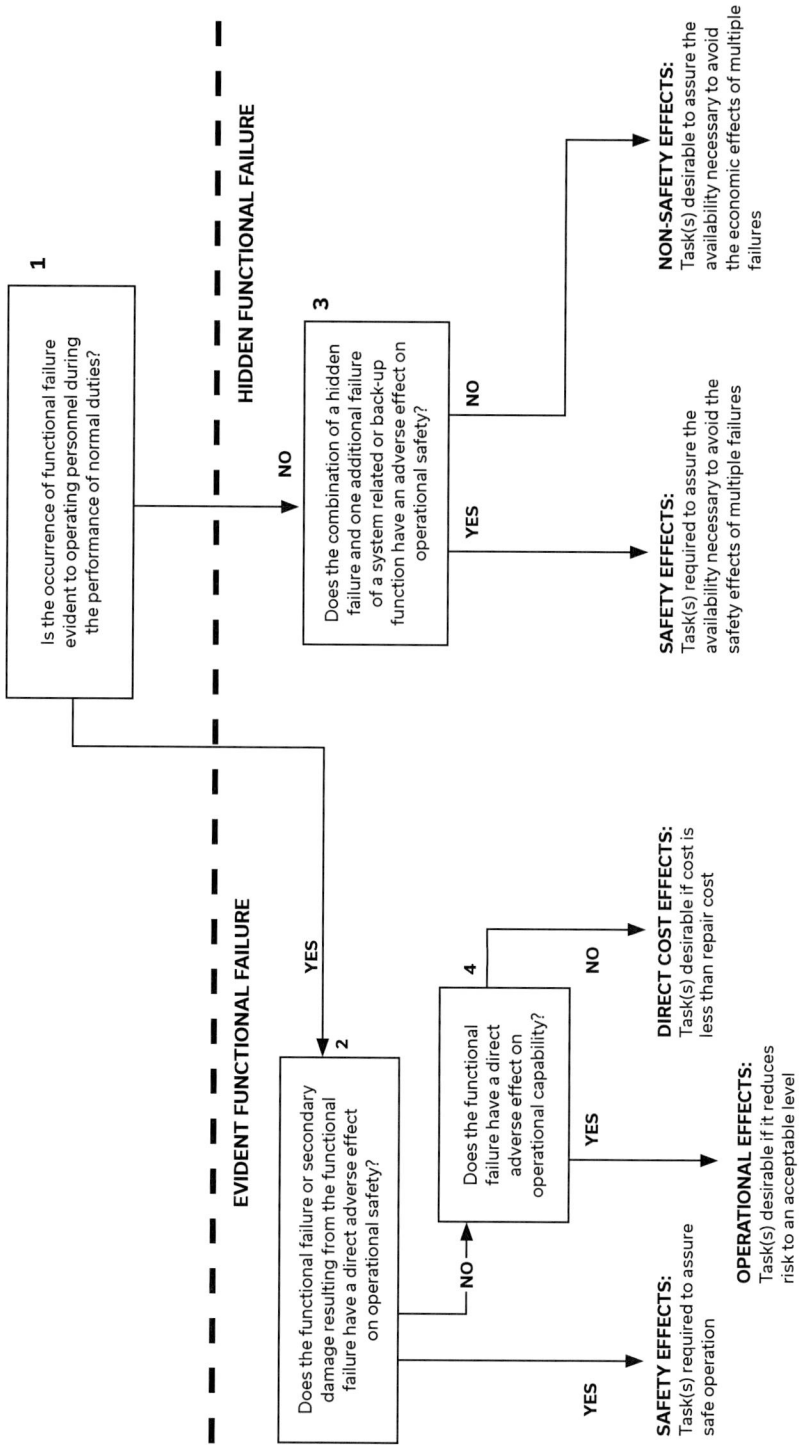

Figure 3.4: Reliability decision logic tree level 1 effects of functional failures

QUESTION 1: Evident or hidden functional failure? The purpose of this question is to segregate the evident and hidden functional failures. This question should be asked for each functional failure.

QUESTION 2: Direct adverse effects on operating safety? To be direct, the functional failure or resulting secondary damage should achieve its effect by itself, not in combination with other functional failures. An adverse effect on operating safety implies that damage or loss of equipment, human injury, death, or some combination of these events is a likely consequence of the failure or resulting secondary damage.

QUESTION 3: Hidden functional failure safety effect? This question takes into account failures in which the loss of a hidden function (i.e., the failure is unknown to the operating personnel) does not in itself affect safety, but in combination with an additional functional failure, has an adverse effect on operating safety.

NOTE: The operating personnel consists of all qualified staff who are on duty and directly involved in the use of the equipment.

QUESTION 4: Direct adverse effect on operating capability? This question asks if the functional failure could have an adverse effect on operating capability by:

- ▶ Requiring either the imposition of operating restrictions or correction prior to further operation; or
- ▶ Requiring operating personnel to use abnormal or emergency procedures.

Second Level Analysis (Effects Categories) (Figure 3.5)

Applying the decision logic of the first level questions to each functional failure leads to one of five effect categories, as follows:

Evident safety effects – This category should be approached with the understanding that a task(s) is required to ensure safe operation. All questions in this category need to be asked. If no applicable and effective task results from this category analysis, then redesign is mandatory.

What Is Reliability Based Preventive Maintenance?

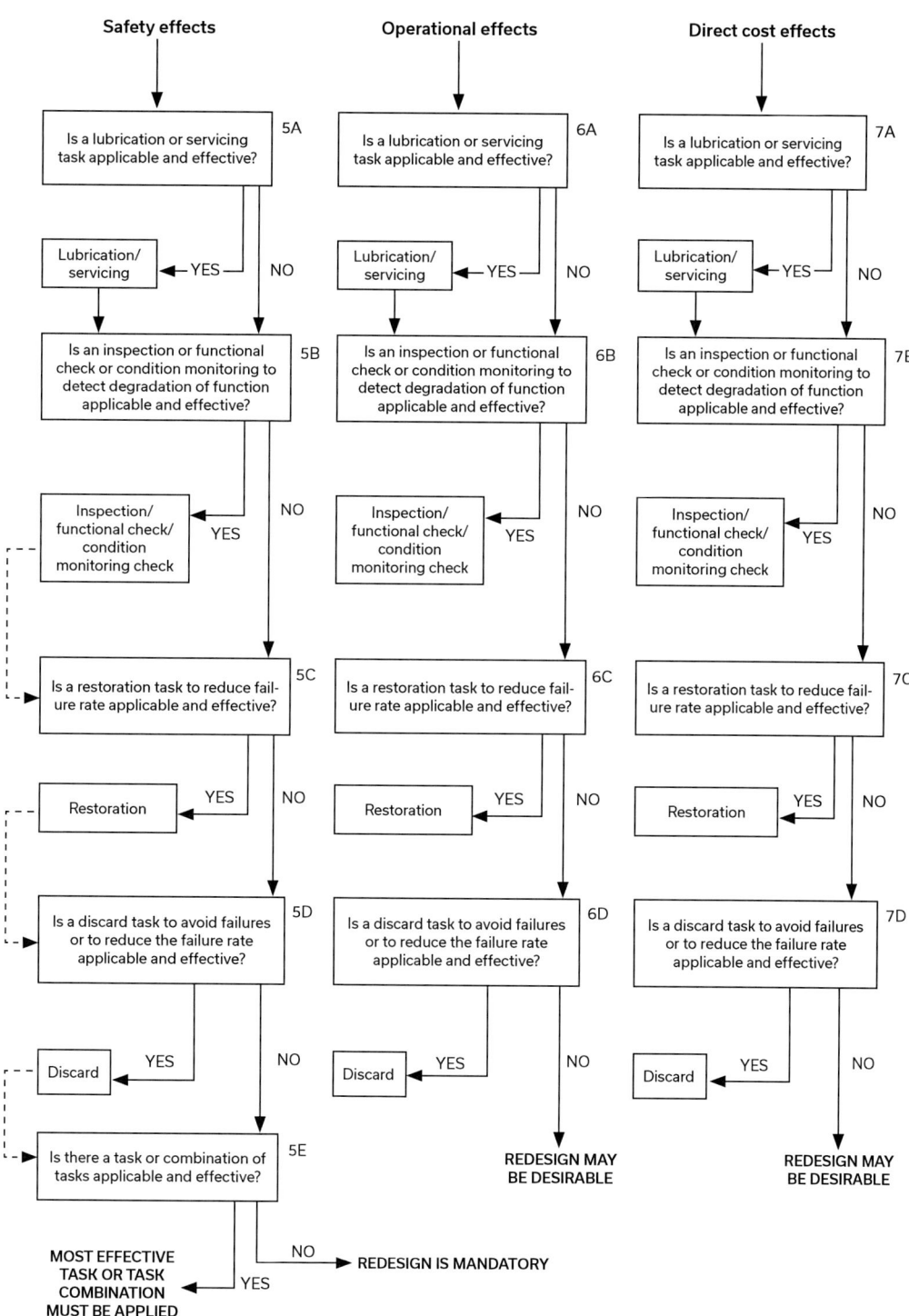

Figure 3.5: Reliability decision logic tree level 2 effects categories and task determination

Evident operational effects – A task is desirable if it reduces the risk of failure to an acceptable level. If all answers are "NO" in the logic process, no preventive maintenance task is generated. If operational penalties are severe, a redesign is desirable.

Evident direct cost effects – A task is desirable if the cost of the task is less than the cost of the repair. If all answers are "NO" in the logic process, no preventive maintenance task is generated. If the cost penalties are severe, a redesign may be desirable.

Hidden function safety effects – The hidden function safety effect requires a task to ensure the availability necessary to avoid the safety effect of multiple failures. All questions should be asked. If no applicable and effective tasks are found, then redesign is mandatory.

Hidden function non-safety effects – This category indicates that a task may be desirable to assure the availability necessary to avoid the direct cost effects of multiple failures. If all answers are "NO" in the logic process, no preventive maintenance task is generated. If economic penalties are severe, a redesign may be desirable.

Task Determination

Task determination is handled in a similar manner for each of the five effect categories. For task determination, it is necessary to apply the failure causes for the functional failure to the second level of the logic diagram. Seven possible task resultant questions in the effect categories have been identified, although additional tasks, modified tasks, or modified task definitions may be warranted, depending on the needs of particular industries.

Paralleling and Default Logic

Paralleling and default logic play an essential role at Level 2. (see Figure 3.5) Regardless of the answer to the first question concerning lubrication/servicing, the next task selection question should be asked in all cases. When following the hidden or evident safety effects path, all subsequent questions should be asked. In the remaining categories, subsequent to the first question, a "YES" answer will allow exiting the logic.

NOTE: At the user's option, advancement is allowable to subsequent questions after a "YES" answer is derived, but only if the cost of the task is equal to the cost of the failure prevented.

Default logic is reflected in paths outside the safety effects areas by the arrangement of the task selection logic. In the absence of adequate information to answer "YES" or "NO" to questions in the second level, default logic dictates that a "NO" answer be given and the subsequent questions be asked. As "NO" answers are generated, the only choice available is the next question, which, in most cases, provides a more conservative, stringent and/or costly route.

Redesign is mandatory for failures that fall into the safety effects category, evident or hidden, and for which there are no applicable and effective tasks.

Maintenance Tasks

Explanations of the terms used in the possible tasks are:

- **Lubrication/servicing (all categories):** This involves any act of lubricating or servicing for maintaining inherent design capabilities.
- **Operational/visual/automated check (hidden functional failure categories only):** An operational check is a task to determine that an item is fulfilling its intended purpose. It does not require quantitative checks and is a failure finding task. A visual check is an observation to determine that an item is fulfilling its intended purpose and does not require quantitative tolerances. This, again, is a failure finding task. The visual check could also involve interrogating electronic units that store failure data.
- **Inspection/functional check/condition monitoring (all categories):** An inspection is an examination of an item against a specific standard. A functional check is a quantitative assessment to determine if one or more functions of an item performs within specified limits. Condition monitoring is a task that may be continuous or periodic to monitor the condition of an item in operation against preset parameters.
- **Restoration (all categories):** Restoration is the work necessary to return the item to a specific standard. Since restoration may vary from cleaning or replacement of single parts up to a complete overhaul, the scope of each assigned restoration task has to be specified.

Chapter 3

TASK	APPLICATION CRITERIA	EFFECTIVENESS CRITERIA		
		SAFETY	OPERATIONAL	DIRECT COST
LUBRICATION OR SERVICING	The replenishment of the consumable shall reduce the rate of functional deterioration.	The task shall reduce the risk of failure.	The task shall reduce the risk of failure to an acceptable level.	The task shall be cost-effective.
OPERATIONAL, VISUAL OR AUTOMATED CHECK	Identification of the failure shall be possible.	The task shall ensure adequate availability of the hidden function to reduce the risk of multiple failure.	Not applicable	The task shall ensure adequate availability of the hidden function in order to avoid economic effects of multiple failures and shall be cost-effective.
INSPECTION, FUNCTIONAL CHECK OR CONDITION MONITORING	Reduced resistance to failure shall be detectable and rate of reduction in failure resistance shall be predictable.	The task shall reduce the risk of failure to assure safe operation.	The task shall reduce the risk of failure to an acceptable level.	The task shall be cost-effective; i.e. the cost of the task shall be less than the cost of the failure prevented.
RESTORATION	The item shall show functional degradation characteristics at an identifiable age and a large proportion of units shall survive to that age. It shall be possible to restore the item to a specific standard of failure resistance.	The task shall reduce the risk of failure to assure safe operation.	The task shall reduce the risk of failure to an acceptable level	The task shall be cost-effective; i.e. the cost of the task shall be less than the cost of the failure prevented.
DISCARD	The item shall show functional degradation characteristics at an identifiable age and a large proportion of units shall survive to that age.	A safe-life limit shall reduce the risk of failure to assure safe operation.	The task shall reduce the risk of failure to an acceptable level.	An economic life limit shall be cost-effective; i.e. the cost of the task shall be less than the cost of the failures prevented.

Table 3.1: Task selection criteria

> ▶ **Discard (all categories):** Discard is the removal from service of an item at a specified life limit. Discard tasks are normally applied to so called single cell parts, such as cartridges, canisters, cylinders, turbine disks, safe life structural members, etc.
> ▶ **Combination (safety categories):** Since this is a safety category question and a task is required, all possible avenues should be analyzed. To do this, a review of the tasks that are applicable is necessary. From this review, the most effective tasks should be selected.
> ▶ **No task (all categories):** It may be decided that no task is required in some situations, depending on the effect.

Each of these possible tasks is based on its own applicability and effectiveness criteria. Table 3.1 summarizes the task selection criteria.

Task Frequencies/Intervals

In order to set a task frequency or interval, it is necessary to determine the existence of applicable operational experience data that suggests an effective interval for task accomplishment. Appropriate information may be obtained from one or more of these:

- ▶ Prior knowledge from other similar equipment that shows a scheduled maintenance task has offered substantial evidence of being applicable, effective and economically worthwhile;
- ▶ Manufacturer/supplier test data that indicates a scheduled maintenance task will be applicable and effective for the item being evaluated;
- ▶ Reliability data and predictions.

Safety and cost considerations need to be addressed when establishing the maintenance intervals. Scheduled inspections and replacement intervals should coincide whenever possible and tasks should be grouped to reduce the operational impact.

A safety replacement interval can be established from the cumulative failure distribution for the item by choosing a replacement interval that results in an extremely low probability of failure prior to replacement. Where a failure does not cause a safety hazard but causes loss of availability, the replacement interval is established in a trade-off process involving the cost of replacement components, the cost of failure and the availability requirement of the equipment.

Mathematical models exist for determining task frequencies and intervals, but these models depend on the availability of the appropriate data. This data will be specific to particular industries and those industry standards and data sheets should be consulted as appropriate.

If there is insufficient reliability data, no prior knowledge from other similar equipment, or insufficient similarity between the previous and current systems, the task interval frequency only can be established initially by experienced personnel using good judgment and operating experience in concert with the best available operating data and relevant cost maintenance and production data.

CHAPTER 4

Enhanced Sensory PM Inspections

Figure 4.1: Vibration reading on a pump

Over the past several years, technology has advanced and introduced several new tools to the world of maintenance reliability. These tools have drastically enhanced the overall effectiveness and efficiency of sensory inspections. Let's take a look at some of these tools and some of the inspection applications for which they are best suited. In order to have a truly effective PM program, you need to utilize a wide variety of tools available to perform these enhanced sensory inspections. When used properly, they all complement each other in one way or another, giving the end user an enormous amount of usable data to make quick, educated decisions on asset management.

The **digital camera** has become so readily available these days in a vast array of models, from basic ones like those on smartphones and tablets to some very elaborate models.

The digital camera can be used in several different inspection applications, such as:

▶ Shafts – By taking close-up shots, a picture can aid planners in identifying what needs to be added to a job plan based on the condition found in a photograph.

Chapter 4

- ▶ Couplings – Excellent visual aid in detecting coupling separation or degradation.
- ▶ Structural cracks – Easily monitored and evaluated through pictures.
- ▶ Identification – The camera is a great tool for identifying loose parts, lubricant leaks and damaged seals, as well as missing parts/components.

CAUTION: When using a camera around any moving or rotating objects as part of an inspection, the end user needs to exercise caution in the placement of the camera to avoid interfering with the equipment or putting one's self in the line of fire. Be sure to use a breakaway wrist strap when using the camera in close proximity to moving objects.

Depending on the surrounding conditions, the camera's flash should be deactivated and a flashlight used to illuminate the part or object. When taking pictures of rotating or moving objects, like a coupling, it may require the technician to take several shots to properly capture the area of interest. The use of a diffuser may be required to aid in removing the flash effect on reflective surfaces.

Another use of the digital camera is for before and after pictures to attach to job plans to show technicians what good looks like. On that note, a digital camera makes a great reference tool for housekeeping after a job is performed. It is definitely true that a picture is worth a thousand words and is an incredible addition to inspections and follow-up findings.

Figure 4.2: The industrial multimeter *(reproduced with permission from Fluke Corporation)*

The **multimeter** is typically used in maintenance and troubleshooting to gather electrical measurements to assess equipment condition. The multimeter is often referred to as the first line of defense in monitoring the condition of electrical equipment. It is used to measure voltage, amperage and continuity, and based on the model of the meter being used, several other related readings. There are several types of specialty meters for specific readings that complement PM programs.

The **videoscope and borescope** are great tools in this category and have come a long way in the past few years with options, such as a digital still camera, video display and recording features.

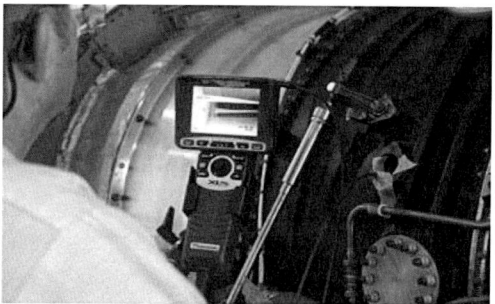

Figure 4.3: Internal inspection using a videoscope

The borescope is basically an extension of the human eye. It has a lens that protrudes through an opening that allows internal inspections on a variety of objects. Although the images captured from a borescope are helpful in detecting defects and imperfections, it is often difficult to determine the actual size of a defect due to the fact that the distance to the defect is often a variable.

Borescopes are available in either a rigid or flexible design, with both having advantages.

- ▶ Borescopes are very useful when used for inspections of gearboxes, turbines and shafts that are internally mounted and not easily accessible to the technician's eye.
- ▶ A borescope can be inserted through a valve or other fitting opening to conduct internal inspections of boiler tubes, fire protection piping, or other piping applications where it is neither feasible nor possible to cut open a section.

CAUTION:

- ▶ When using a borescope for such inspections, be careful when inserting the scope to avoid damaging the camera lens or optic end of the scope. Detection and classification of defects with a borescope is generally considered a specialized skill that requires training in the methods and procedures utilized in inspections.
- ▶ Do not use a borescope or videoscope on components or equipment while in operation. Safety for the individual is always first.

Strobe lights are specialty lights designed to emit a flash of light at an adjustable rate to make a rotating object appear to be standing still or even rotate backwards for ease of inspection.

Some strobe lights, which can be specially designed and calibrated, are capable of flashing up to hundreds of times per second, giving them the ability to make the object of interest appear to be stopped. This is particularly beneficial when inspecting rotating objects, such as sheaves, pulleys and belts, or chains attached to these, without having to shut down production to inspect. With a strobe light, you are able to detect whether the belts are tensioned properly, damaged, cracked, or glazed. Strobe lights are also great for inspecting couplings for worn teeth or cracks, tears and loose or missing bolts. You can also perform run time inspections on motors to check for dirty, damaged, or missing cooling fans. The strobe light also allows inspections of key length, key engagement, key condition and key offset, which should be approximately 180 degrees. On general equipment, you can also identify structural or mechanical looseness, cracks, fractures, structural deflection and structural mode shape.

A stroboscopic effect is created or adjusted when a known marked point or spot on the rotating object appears to move backward, forward, or not moving at all. Movement depends on the frequency of the strobe flash. If the flash happens when it is equal to the period of the rotation, the object will look like it is not moving. If adjustments are made and a non-integer flash setting is applied, it will make the mark appear to move forward or backward.

For example, if a slight increase of flash frequency is adjusted, the mark will appear to be rotating backward. Alternatively, if the adjustment is made by decreasing the flash frequency, the object would appear to be going forward.

When using a strobe light for shaft inspections, ensure the strobe or flash setting is matched to the shaft speed.

CAUTION:

- ▶ The use of strobe lights may induce an epileptic seizure among individuals who are prone to this type of medical condition.
- ▶ When using these instruments, always be aware of your surroundings as rapidly moving/rotating objects may appear to be stationary.

Infrared spot radiometers are another necessary tool in every technician's toolbox. They can be used anywhere and easily identify an issue by monitoring temperature without the expense of a thermal imager.

There are a few factors to keep in mind when using these devices:

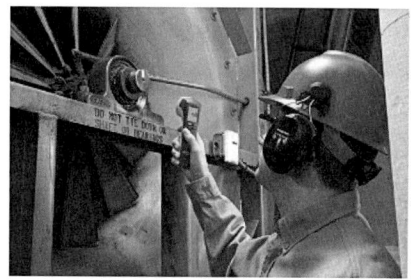

Figure 4.4: Infrared spot radiometers *(reproduced with permission from Fluke Corporation)*

- Ensure that the emissivity is set to match the surface that is to be measured.
- The target area on the object being observed should be larger than the spot size of the radiometer because distance from the target greatly affects accuracy with these tools.
- When pointing the radiometer at the target, you should keep the angle to your target as close to 90 degrees as possible.
- It is a good practice to have targets permanently marked on the objects to ensure accuracy and repeatability.
- Make sure the surface is not reflective, such as a shiny stainless steel. Flat black paint can be used in non-food grade areas for spots where temperatures will be measured on a regular basis. This step eliminates the need to adjust the radiometer's emissivity.
- Infrared spot radiometers are great for performing follow-up corrective work found during a thermographic PM as a baseline if you do not have a thermal imager.
- Common inspection applications for the radiometer are electric motors, bearings, belts, mechanical seals, couplings, gearboxes, lube/hydraulic reservoirs and associated piping, heat exchangers and steam traps.
- Maintenance reliability and operations personnel should have easy access to these handy little tools as they are relatively inexpensive and easy to use, especially in the absence of a formal IR thermographic program.

Ultrasound, ultrasonic detection and inspections are part of an enhanced sensory inspections category that is starting to become extremely popular, and for good reasons. They are an integral part of condition monitoring. These detection instruments cover a large envelope of objects/equipment and marry well with other technologies, such as vibration analysis and monitoring.

The ultrasound instruments, often called translators, are relatively simple to use and are comprised of an handheld unit with a set of headphones, a display panel with sensitivity adjustment and most models also come with interchangeable modules and attachments for measuring in either airborne or structure borne mode.

Although these instruments are relatively easy to use, there is a certain amount of training required to be able to gauge the intensity of sonic patterns and hear the ultrasounds that are produced by different pieces of equipment.

The advantage of these instruments is that they can hear changes in equipment through the ultrasounds and directional characteristics of these sounds and warn of an imminent failure before there is an actual failure. Quite often, these ultrasound instruments can detect problems before they are detected by either vibration or infrared.

The most common applications for ultrasound tend to fall into four categories:

1. **Mechanical:** All mechanical equipment produces a sound signature while operating. When equipment is operating properly, it gives off a distinct sound signature. The signature at this point is called normal. When a failure has started within a component, that sound signature will make a noticeable change from the normal signature. This shift in intensity will be visible on the display panel of the tool and the technician will hear the difference through the headphones. These sound snapshots or samples can be reviewed or analyzed through the use of what is called spectral analysis software on the technician's computer. Inspection applications for mechanical inspections are compressor valves leaks, bearings, gearboxes and cavitation in pumps.

2. **Electrical:** Usually, infrared is used for checking electrical components for heat signatures that indicate certain failures. However, the use of ultrasound will detect sound signatures that are an early warning sound for an impending failure.

Motor Rebuilds/Purchases
for years (2010-2012)

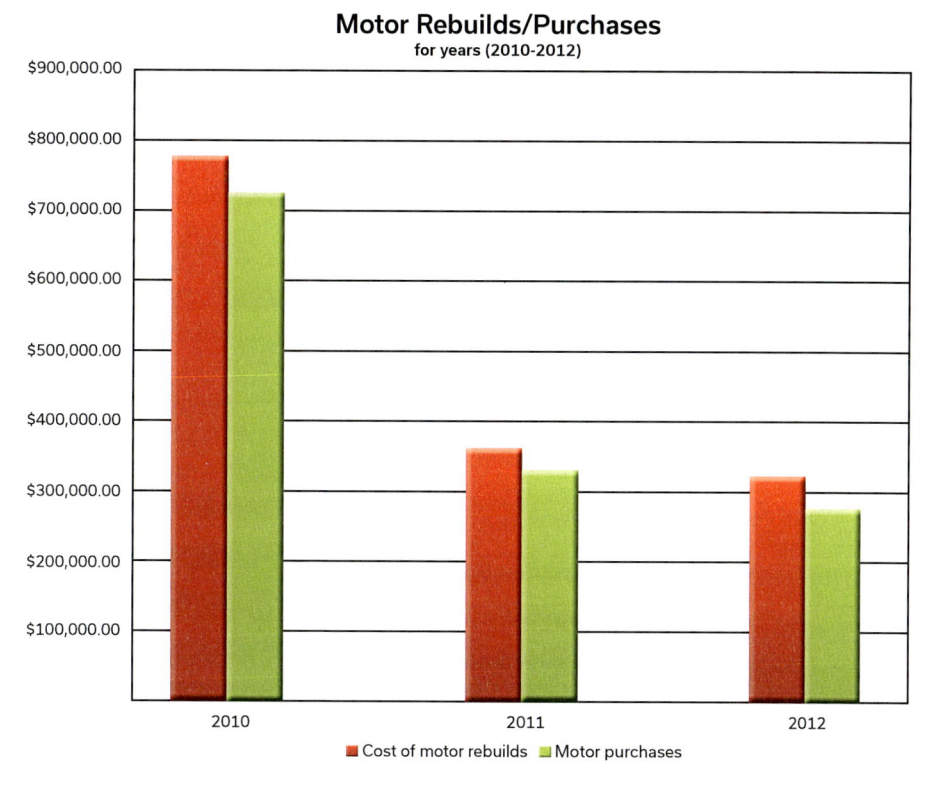

[Bar chart showing Cost of motor rebuilds and Motor purchases for years 2010, 2011, and 2012. In 2010, rebuilds ~$775,000 and purchases ~$725,000. In 2011, rebuilds ~$355,000 and purchases ~$325,000. In 2012, rebuilds ~$315,000 and purchases ~$270,000.]

Figure 4.5: Results from use of ultrasound lubrication and laser alignment over 3 years

CAUTION: There are a few problems that, if gone undetected, could result in a serious arc flash incident. When inspecting for these, the technician will attach a parabolic dish to the ultrasound instrument, which allows for a greater and safer distance from the actual test point. These often potentially destructive events are known as arcing, corona, mechanical looseness and tracking.

3. **Leak Detection:** Ultrasound is an extremely versatile diagnostic tool for pinpointing leaks in air compressors, steam traps and many other applications. Ultrasound detection instruments are especially helpful when implementing an energy conservation program and detecting air leaks since this is one of the most expensive utilities often overlooked or overshadowed by other issues.

4. **Lubrication:** One of the most common causes of bearing failures is attributed to improper lubrication practices. The use of ultrasound has altered the time-based preventive maintenance to a more predictive concept. *Talk about PM optimization!*

This is a quick win to implement into your lube program. By training the technicians to listen to and view the spectral analysis of bearings on their routes, they will be able to identify only those bearings that require lubrication, leaving those that do not alone until lubrication is required. The training provided enables the technician to apply only the amount of lubricant necessary so the problem of over or under lubricating is effectively eliminated.

Figure 4.6: Application of lubrication using ultrasound *(photo courtesy of UE Systems)*

Simple vibration meters, vibe pens and complex vibration analyzers are tools capable of measuring vibration caused by a structural or rotational defect, as well as detecting bearing or gear mesh issues found in higher frequencies. This is especially helpful when the contractor who normally performs your routes is several hours away.

Vibration analysis is a complex process that requires significant time, money and effort to become extremely proficient in it. A lot of organizations tend to outsource their vibration analysis program and cover their critical assets on a set interval of inspections. By training your own technicians to use a vibe pen or even a slightly more advanced handheld vibration meter, you have the ability to make some hard go/no-go decisions at a moment's notice.

Figure 4.7: Technician using vibration analysis tool *(reproduced with permission from Fluke Corporation)*

Another perfect use of these tools is to act as check and baseline gathering devices for when a pump, motor, or gearbox has been changed out and needs to be monitored for a period of time to verify that out of alignment, soft foot and other related issues are not present. The technicians can then provide the data they collected to the contractor for reference against that asset. Some of these handheld meters come with vibration and temperature measuring capabilities that can be invaluable to the technician out in the field.

Thermal Imaging or IR Cameras take images that are not visible to the human eye since our eyes only see in the visible light spectrum as electromagnetic radiation not infrared radiation. All objects that have a temperature above absolute zero, which is a staggering −273 degrees Celsius, give off radiation in the infrared zone or region. Infrared radiation is around us daily in such forms as sunlight or fire.

Because of our inability to see infrared radiation, our bodies tend to feel it through our skin and nerves as heat. So using these thermal imagers or cameras turns what is typically invisible to the human eye visible. This is what make them one of the better tools for predicting failures. These cameras are used for looking at larger areas than those examined by spot radiometers and can easily identify problems that the spot radiometer would have missed. There are several industrial applications in which thermal imaging cameras are extremely useful.

EXAMPLE 1:
Steam leaking through closed steam trap

EXAMPLE 2:
TPM production personnel monitoring temperature of process

Electrical installations: Thermal imaging cameras are used for both low and high voltage installation. There are several failures these cameras can detect, such as loose or improperly installed connections, overheated components or connections, short circuit situations, defects within insulators and oxidation of switches. If not detected soon enough, all these failures could result in significant asset failure and possible fire situations.

Chapter 4

Certain applications and measurement tools can take the data they collected and transmit the results to your smartphone or tablet. This allows the technician to immediately share data with a supervisor or co-worker and perform comparisons to previously recorded data. Once again, the tools and options to develop a solid program are limited only by one's imagination, determination and, of course, budget. The key is to establish the best program available with the resources you are provided.

This chapter does not cover all the available enhanced sensory inspection tools that are on the market as the list is extremely extensive. Rather, it is written to give you an understanding of the wide variety of options from which to choose.

Figure 4.8: Example of new infrared technologies available *(reproduced with permission from Fluke Corporation)*

No matter how simple or complex or asset intensive your operation is, one thing is for sure – you need to have the ability to perform your PM program while adding value to your bottom line. By incorporating a mix of enhanced sensory inspection tools into your program, you will be able to marry a lot of the technologies into one inspection route and reduce the amount of time your technicians would normally spend doing otherwise invasive inspection techniques that typically introduce more risk. By creating more run time inspections, you can better plan and schedule repairs rather than prolong an outage fixing what was found at that time.

CHAPTER 5

Writing Effective Work Procedures

As with most things in life, humans tend to do what is asked of them. That is why it is imperative to develop solid, repeatable procedures to be followed when performing any type of maintenance, whether it's preventive or corrective. If you were to ask one of your millwrights to go out and check the conveyor without providing further details, imagine what level of detail the report would entail.

These days, many companies are faced with a shortage of skilled trades as they watch the tribal knowledge of their seasoned craftspeople walk out the door upon retirement. This is why you need to develop solid and concise procedures that will capture the data necessary to allow you to make informed decisions on when and how to intervene with an asset.

Writing an Effective PM Work Procedure

Maintenance professionals are often measured on work execution effectiveness, which measures how well they execute the work they are assigned, be it PM, PdM, or corrective maintenance.

There are templates that give you a sequence to follow, which is great, but it is what you enter into the template that is critical to the effectiveness of the procedure. The true value of having effective PM procedures is that they make the work measurable and allow a task to be carried out by a number of different people, yet yield the same results. This shortens the learning curve with newly hired people and removes the fear of losing that tribal knowledge when people leave. By implementing standards of work execution, you, in turn, improve the reliability of your assets and your processes.

In order to create an effective procedure for any type of work, the job plan must include step-by-step procedures with the following information:

- Any and all safety/cautionary warnings, lockout-tagout procedures, hazard assessments, etc.
- Standards or specifications to be followed.
- Any special permitting requirements, such as hot work, confined space, etc.
- Whether the procedure should be carried out while the equipment/machine is running, shut down, or normal mode of operation.
- The frequency of the PM and PdM, such as quarterly, biweekly, etc., as well as the expected duration of the procedure.
- A list of the craft or suitability and the number of personnel needed to accomplish the procedure. For example: "2 Mechanics @ 2.5 hrs. ea., 1 Electrician @ 1.0 hrs. ea." Make sure to add all required resources to the procedure if others are required.
- The estimated time to complete a PM, including any setup time, lockout-tagout and prep time as accurately as possible.
- A list of parts required to complete the task, including special tools or equipment, such as a 1/2-inch drive torque wrench, a 60-foot man lift, etc.
- Include photos to a procedure for added clarity. As the old adage states, "A picture is worth a thousand words."
- An area on the procedure to document actual findings so they can be recorded in the computerized maintenance management system (CMMS) for historical purposes. For example, a procedure asks, "Is the chain stretched?" The people performing the inspections or corrections are provided with the appropriate tool to check the actual chain stretch, some range of what's acceptable and a place to provide feedback.
- Any special instructions that are required.

The following template is simple, yet effective, and may be modified to suit any need.

WORK PROCEDURE TEMPLATE

Work Procedure PM Template	TYPE: **PM Inspection** **Equipment Shutdown**
Provide a detailed account of activities in order of execution to provide concise direction with any specialty tools and any and all safety warnings.	Frequency requested: **Quarterly-**

ASSET Name-Number	Functional Location
Overhead Acceleration Chain Conveyor – **30126611**	**0177-53130-00010-01702**

PM Task(s) Description(s)	Suitability or Craft Requirement
1-Visually Inspect Chain Wear	Millwright X 2 @ 1.0 hours
2-Visually Inspect Chain Attachments	Millwright X 2 @ 1.0 hours

NOTE
Parts only will be required if inspection findings warrant change out. If change out is required, write a PM07 for the corrective work using parts listed below. If parts are not used, they must be returned to stores. Document all findings on the work order.

Parts Required (#)	Parts Description	Quantity	Kitting Required?
14087599	LH Chain Dog w/Conn.	4	Yes
14087600	RH Chain Dog w/Conn.	4	Yes
14102228	Connecting Link – Offset	2	Yes
14102229	Connecting Link-60-2R	2	Yes
14102230	Chain-RLR-60-2R	2	Yes

Specialty Tool Requirements:
12" Pry Bar, 3' Ladder, Impact Gun and 1/2" Socket, Needle-Nose Pliers, Chain Break Link Tool, FB Chain Stretch Gauge, Oxyacetylene Torch Kit No Mobile/Man Lift Equipment required for this task
Special Planning/Scheduling Requirements:
Equipment shutdown; Operations to clean off conveyor
Special References to Note:
SAP Job Plan 16672-M3A, Acceleration Chain
SAP Job Plan 02546-OP3A, Acceleration Chain to Pre-Loader Cleanup

Chapter 5

Step #	Step Description and Information	Suitability	# Required	Estimated Time (hours)
1	**Prep for Chain Inspection**			
	CAUTION Ensure Operations has completed cleanup prior to beginning PM.			
1.A	Jog conveyor until at least one master link is visible and accessible on top	MW	2	0.15
1.A.1	Lockout-Tagout and test fire acceleration chain conveyor	MW	2	0.15
	WARNING Company employee must lock-out and verify zero energy. Also verify any contractor lockout prior to commencing any work. Failure to do so could lead to serious injury or death. Any violations will be treated as a lockout violation.			
1.A.2	Use ladder to access the forming line belt at north end of nose joint to begin PM	MW	2	0.125
1.B	**Chain Inspection**			
1.B.1	Loosen chain take up using impact gun and 1/2" socket	MW	1	0.125
	NOTE **Chain must be loosened off enough to get the top section out of the raceway.**			
1.B.2	Using the 12" pry bar, remove chain from raceway. Remove about a 10' section.	MW	2	0.15
1.B.3	Check for play in chain side to side and length ways; Document any abnormalities	MW	2	0.30
1.B.4	Check for uneven and excessive wear in barrels and side bars; Document findings	MW	2	0.30
1.B.5	Inspect UHMW raceway for wear and note for future work; Document findings	MW	2	0.125

Step #	Step Description and Information	Suitability	# Required	Estimated Time (hours)
1.C	**Removing Links**			
	NOTE Chain stretch is to be taken 10" from the take up. Using the FB chain gauge, measure for stretch. If chain is stretched or elongated more than 6%, it needs to be changed. Chain can only be shortened once by removing links before new chain must be installed.			
1.C.1	Check chain stretch and document findings	MW	2	0.15
1.C.2	Remove master link and separate the chain	MW	2	0.15
1.C.3	Opposite end can be separated using the chain break tool or a torch	MW	2	0.25
1.C.4	Install new master link in chain	MW	1	0.15
	NOTE Ensure all pins are installed so they face outward for cotter pin access.			
2.A	**Dog/Attachment Inspection**			
2.A.1	Check for uneven wear on mating surface	MW	2	0.30
2.A.2	Rotate and or move dogs back and forth to check for excessive play	MW	2	0.30
2.B	**Installing New Dogs/Attachments**			
2.B.1	Remove existing cotter pin	MW	2	0.50
2.B.2	Use the chain tool to push out the pin	MW	2	0.30
2.B.3	Remove old dog/attachment	MW	2	0.15

Chapter 5

Step #	Step Description and Information	Suitability	# Required	Estimated Time (hours)
2.C	**Installing New Attachments**			
2.C.1	Install new attachments facing head shaft	MW	2	0.10
2.C.2	Insert pin into attachment, connect it to the chain	MW	2	0.30
2.C.3	Install cotter pin and ensure it is bent to avoid falling out	MW	2	0.15
	NOTE All work must be tested prior to returning equipment to operations.			

Condition As Found

Condition As Left

Comments (use back of form if more room is required)

Maintenance Tech(s) Signature(s):

_____

Maintenance Supervisor's Signature:

_____

CHAPTER 6

Five Tips for Optimizing a PM Program

Chances are you already know the case for doing preventive maintenance is airtight. Done right, PM will preserve, protect and extend the life of your equipment.

So here's the question: Why are so many maintenance reliability professionals unhappy with their PM programs?

The two biggest complaints are:

1. PM consumes too many resources.
2. The results of PM are not what was expected.

Figure 6.1: Trying to make sense of it all

A PM program can be optimized by following five recommendations. These "5 Tips for Optimizing Your PM Program" are based on years of working in maintenance reliability. These tips are not what should be accomplished in order to optimize your PM program, but are known best practices.

PM Optimization Tip #1: Measure the effectiveness of your PM program

"You can't manage what you can't measure."
– W. Edwards Deming

Chapter 6

There are a few metrics or measurements one can use to measure effectiveness of a current PM program.

The simplest measurement one can use to identify whether a current PM program is effective is "PM Labor Hours vs. Emergency/Urgent Labor Hours." Urgent labor is included with emergency labor hours because one should use a known standard definition for a failure. The definition used is taken from the December 29, 1978 Reliability Centered Maintenance Study by F. Stanley Nowlan and Howard F. Heap.

> *Failure – An unsatisfactory condition which is unacceptable to the end user.*

Using this definition of a failure, any work done that is not preventive or predictive maintenance would be considered a failure.

When put on a line graph together, these two measurements provide a facility manager with a clear picture of the effectiveness of a current PM program. Check out the graphs in Figures 6.2 and 6.3. Both these graphs came from different facilities and tell different stories.

PM Labor Hour vs. EM/Urgent Labor Hours

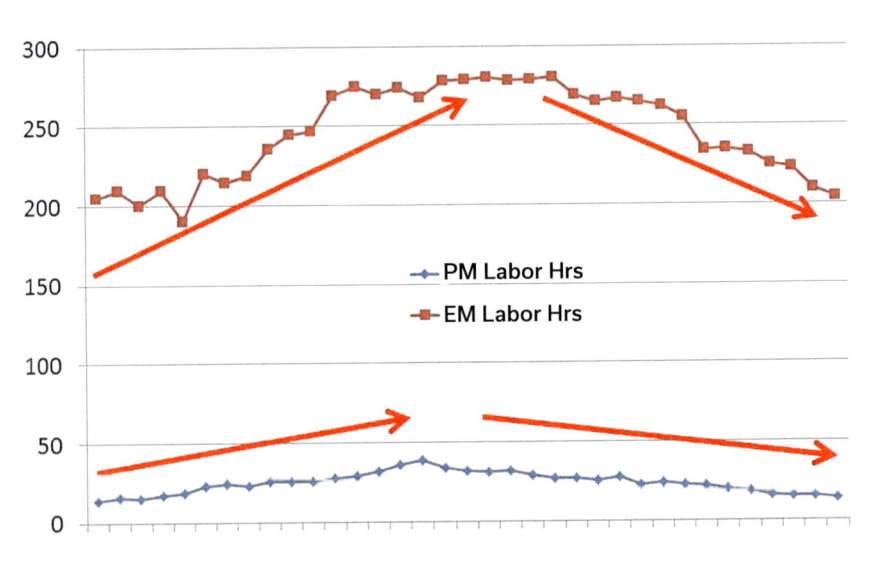

Figure 6.2: Example of measuring PM program effectiveness

44

Five Tips for Optimizing a PM Program

In Figure 6.2, PM labor hours are shown through circles, while emergency/urgent labor hours are shown through squares. What is interesting about this graph is that as PM labor hours increase, so do emergency/urgent labor hours. This is not what one would expect from a PM program that is rock solid. What would be expected is that as PM labor hours increase, emergency/urgent labor hours decrease. As for the facility manager, which is shown in Figure 6.3, the decision was made to evaluate and optimize PMs by starting with the most critical ones and to continue measuring PM versus emergency/urgent labor hours.

PM Effectiveness
PM Labor Hours vs. Emergency/Urgent Labor Hours

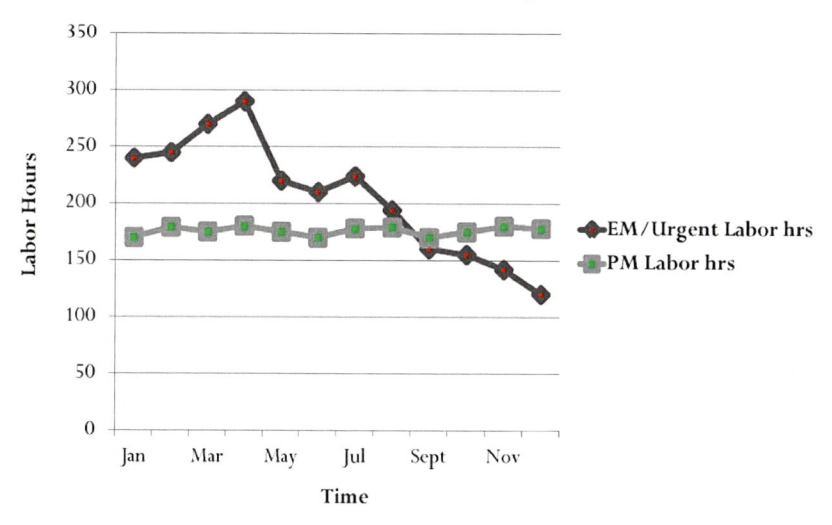

Figure 6.3: Example of PM effectiveness measured program

In Figure 6.3, the emergency/urgent labor hours are decreasing as preventive maintenance labor hours stay consistent. This graph was assembled after the facility manager reviewed and adjusted the PM program. The PMs became more focused on the elimination or mitigation of specific failure modes (i.e., how something fails) after the review and modification of PM procedures.

The survey that follows identifies some of the true problems of why a PM program is not effective.

*Rank the effectiveness of your Preventive Maintenance Program.
1 = Never, 2 = Sometimes, 3 = Not Sure, 4 = Unknown, 5 = Yes

Answer	1	2	3	4	5	Number of Responses	Rating Score*
Does your PM/PdM Program focus on Failure Modes?						86	2.5
Do you truly measure PM/PdM Effectiveness?						86	2.2
Do you have inspector and inspection criteria for PM/PdM?						86	2.8
Are the people lubricating equipment qualified or trained?						86	3.3
Does your PM/PdM Program provide positive results over 75% of the time?						86	3.0

*The Rating Score is the weighted average calculated by dividing the sum of all weighted ratings by the number of total responses.

Figure 6.4: Example of poll PM effectiveness questions (poll by Ricky Smith in 2015)

QUESTION 1: Only fifty percent of respondents stated their PM/PdM program is currently focused on specific failure modes.

QUESTION 2: Forty percent of respondents actually measure the effectiveness of their PM/PdM program.

QUESTION 3: Over fifty percent stated they developed inspector and inspection criteria for the PM/PdM program.

QUESTION 4: Over sixty percent stated that the people who conducted lubrication were trained and qualified.

QUESTION 5: Surprisingly, over fifty percent stated their PM/PdM program provides positive results over seventy-five percent of the time.

PM Optimization Tip #2: Preventive maintenance should consume only fifteen to twenty percent of total maintenance labor hours

Preventive maintenance in facilities is key to meeting the requirements of the customer (e.g., facility owners, users, etc.). Therefore, resources must be used effectively and efficiently. Managing preventive maintenance effectively and efficiently, as with all proactive maintenance activities, needs to be planned and scheduled effectively. Planning for preventive maintenance activities includes the following items: labor type, estimated labor hours, material or parts required, inspection procedure, specific tools required, etc. Scheduling for preventive maintenance activities is defined as scheduling all personnel involved in the PM by day and/or by hour. All PM activities should be scheduled at least a week prior to execution. Operations or facility owners should have agreed to the schedule at least a week prior to execution.

If preventive maintenance is not planned and scheduled effectively, maintenance labor, material and contractor costs are higher, by as much as fifty to two hundred percent. Maintenance must have a dedicated planner/scheduler per seven to fifteen maintenance personnel in order to reduce the excessive waste of money and labor. Typical metrics used in maintenance planning and scheduling is percentage of planned work and scheduled compliance by day and/or by week.

PM Optimization Tip #3: Measure PM compliance within ten percent of the time frequency

Measuring PM compliance within ten percent of the time frequency was developed to reduce variation in inspection intervals, human performance and asset reliability. This method is known today as the "10% Rule of Preventive Maintenance."

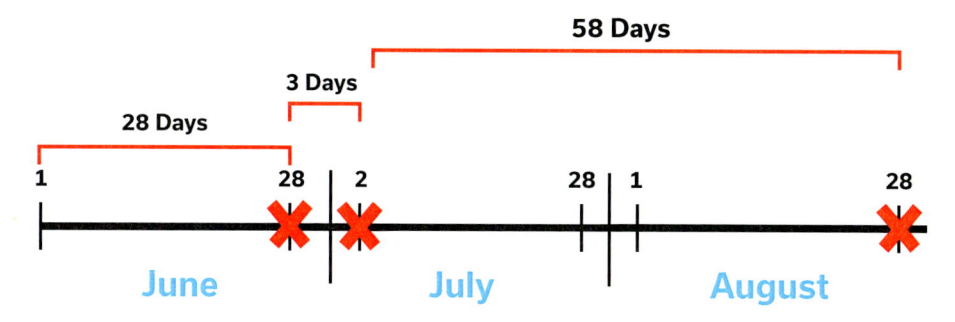

- **30-day PM** - Must be completed within three days or PM is "Out of Compliance"
- **"Out of Compliance"** means more equipment failures and higher maintenance costs because of variation in execution

Figure 6.5: An example of the 10% rule of preventive maintenance

Chapter 6

Here is how the 10% Rule of Preventive Maintenance works: The rule states that if a PM is executed within ten percent of a time frequency, it is considered compliant with the standard. An example would be a monthly PM that must be completed within one and a half days on each side of the due date to be in compliance (use thirty days as an average for a monthly PM calculation). The reason for applying this rule is to reduce the variation of PM execution time frequency. In maintenance, one must identify and reduce variation in the maintenance process and this is a great example where it should be applied.

In the next example, you will see the problem with a typical facility's PM program.

A thirty day PM of XYZ typical facility is executed in June near the end of the month. (There were too many problems at the beginning of June, so the PMs had to be pushed back.)

At the beginning of July, the same PM is executed. (Things were going well at the beginning of the month, so one must complete the PMs because you know bad days are coming).

In August, the PM is executed on the 28th of the month. (Because there were too many problems at the beginning of the month).

After this ninety-day period, the thirty day PM is actually a twenty-eight day PM, a three day PM and a fifty-eight day PM. See the problem? This problem is worse when an organization uses maintenance software or enterprise asset management (EAM) software that kicks out all PMs for the month on the first of the month and you think you have thirty days to complete them. Maintenance crews are told to make sure their PMs are completed within the month so they can meet one hundred percent PM compliance. Can you see the problem now? In many organizations, the focus is on PM compliance rather than stopping failures in their facilities.

PM Optimization Tip #4: Focus preventive maintenance on specific failure modes

Failure modes are defined as how something fails. Let's use a flat membrane roof as an example of what a failure mode is. On a flat membrane roof, one failure mode may be "penetration of roof membrane" and the causes of this failure mode could be many. Knowing the failure mode(s) and cause(s) of a specific

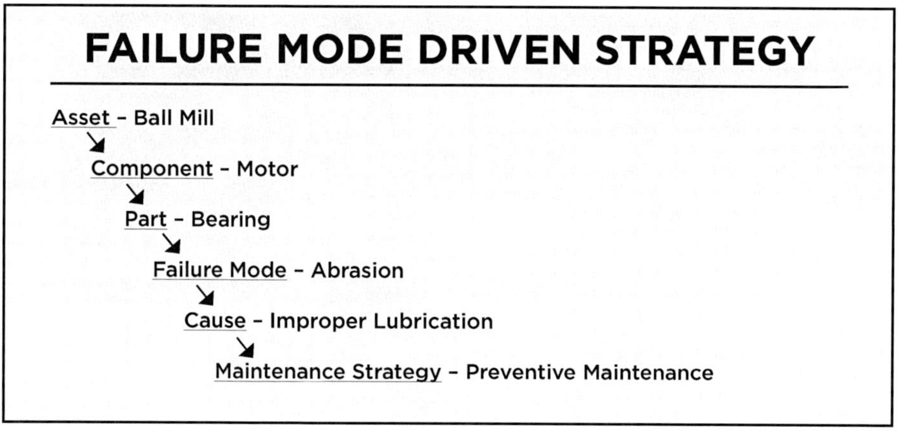

Five Tips for Optimizing a PM Program

FAILURE MODE DRIVEN STRATEGY

Asset - Ball Mill
↘
   Component - Motor
   ↘
      Part - Bearing
      ↘
         Failure Mode - Abrasion
         ↘
            Cause - Improper Lubrication
            ↘
               Maintenance Strategy - Preventive Maintenance

Figure 6.6: Failure mode driven strategy hierarchy

maintainable item, such as a membrane roof, can be key to early detection of roof failure so the repair can be made before it effects an operation.

Another key factor for having the ability to identify the failure mode(s) and cause(s) is it allows a maintenance organization to review the cause(s) of a failure mode and put in place a mitigation strategy, such as not allowing unauthorized personnel on the roof. Once an organization knows the specific failure modes and their causes for maintainable items, unexpected events or failures become a rare occasion.

PM Optimization Tip #5: Predictive maintenance may be the better maintenance strategy

Although predictive maintenance technologies themselves can get quite complicated, the basic concept of PdM is simple enough. Most maintainable items do not suddenly fail. The truth is, maintainable items wear down gradually over a period of weeks or months. Many times, numerous warning signals go off along the way.

These early warning signs, such as slight changes in temperature, vibration, or sound, can be detected by PdM technologies. As a result, PdM gives you time to plan, schedule and make repairs before the maintainable item fails catastrophically or fails without notice, causing serious problems.

Early detection of a failure is key to optimizing reliability of any facility. In Figure 6.7, the P-F curve is a graphic representation of how a part fails, thus

Chapter 6

Potential Failure Curve
Across the Equipment's Lifecycle

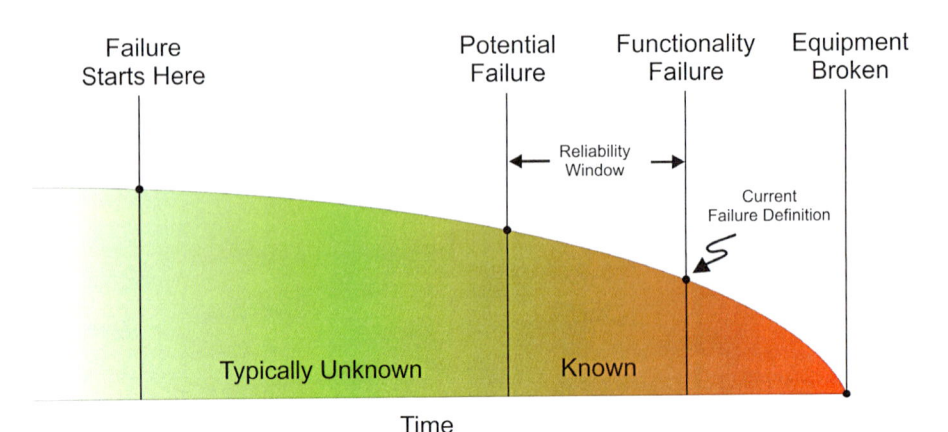

Figure 6.7: The P-F curve

many times causing the equipment to fail. On the P-F curve, "Equipment Condition" is on the left side and the top shows the point at which failure starts to occur and if not corrected, will continue until a total failure occurs. Understanding this P-F curve methodology is only important when failure is unacceptable.

If a failure is unacceptable, then detection of this failure early enough is important so it can be corrected without disruption to an operation. If this is true for a specific failure mode, then one must use the most effective maintenance strategy for early detection. And this strategy would be predictive maintenance (sometimes called condition monitoring), whether using thermography, ultrasound, vibration analysis, motor circuit analysis, etc.

If preventive maintenance is used to detect a failure mode, it typically would be found too far down the P-F curve. Most of the time, failure occurs before action can be taken, causing unexpected problems to an operation.

Consider this: Fifteen to twenty percent of work should be PM, twenty-five to thirty-five percent should be PdM. It is all about the failure modes. Table 6.1 shows world-class maintenance data from the Alcoa Mt. Holly plant, considered one of the best in the world in proactive maintenance for many years. A benchmark study was conducted in the early 1980s (Benchmark #1) and later after the 1990s (Benchmark #2).

Categories	Benchmark #1	Benchmark #2
Maintenance Spending / RAV	3.4%	2.0%
Budget Compliance	-0.5%	+3.7%
Overtime / Straight Time	1.0	7.1%
Number of Crafts	4	3
Planners per Tradesperson	1:20	1:19
Absenteeism	1.6%	1.8%
Backlog in Crew Weeks (Per Tradesperson)	4.4	6.8 Total/6.25 Ready
Schedule Compliance	95%	85.7%
Percent of Urgent (Interruption) Work	10.5%	3%
Percent of PM / PdM to all Work Orders	32%	47.2%
PM Accomplishment	96%	85.7% (10% Rule)
Inventory Accuracy	96%	97.6%
Inventory Turns	3.31	2.86
Maintenance Training $'s as % Total Payroll $	4.2%	1%
Wrench Time	62.3%	58.8%

Table 6.1: Alcoa Mt. Holly plant benchmark data

CHAPTER 7

Preventive Maintenance Metrics

Preventive maintenance does, indeed, impact asset availability through minimizing downtime, mitigating failures and detecting potential failures. If a step in the process is skipped or performed at a substandard level, it creates defects known as failures.

Managing with the right metrics allows maintenance leaders and their team members to see the effect their preventive maintenance program has on equipment reliability.

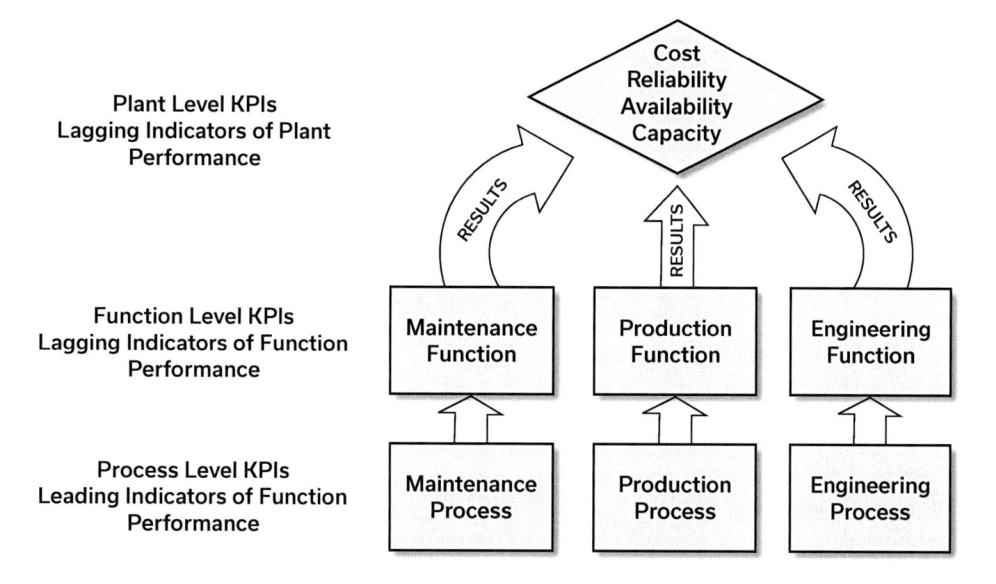

Figure 7.1: Graphical representation of leading and lagging KPI process

53

Chapter 7

Preventive maintenance is critical to managing the reliability of an organization's assets, along with maintenance and operations costs. Leading metrics and/or key performance indicators (KPIs) lead to the results and lagging metrics/KPIs are the results.

EXAMPLE: Preventive Maintenance Leading KPI – PM Compliance

PM compliance can impact emergency labor hours and equipment capacity. Emergency labor hours and equipment capacity are both lagging KPIs.

If PM compliance (leading KPI) was at thirty percent, then failures are probably high and maintenance can measure maintenance emergency labor hours (lagging KPI).

If a PM program is effective and compliance is low, then maintenance emergency labor hours will be high.

Figure 7.2 is an example of leading and lagging KPIs one could use for preventive maintenance.

PM Lagging KPIs:
1. Emergency Labor Hours
2. Maintenance Cost
3. OEE, MTBF, MTTR

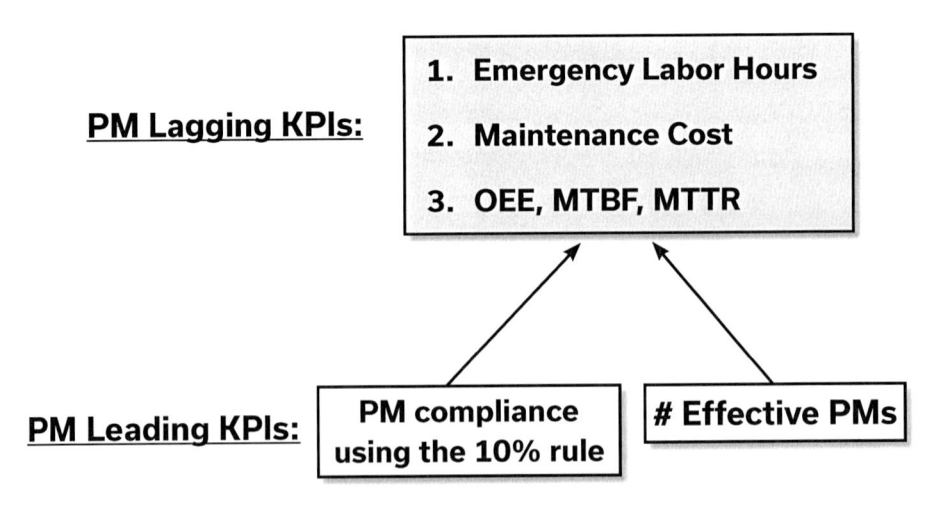

PM Leading KPIs: PM compliance using the 10% rule | # Effective PMs

Figure 7.2: PM leading and PM lagging KPI hierarchy

> **WARNING:** YOU CANNOT CONDUCT PM EFFECTIVELY WITHOUT THE EQUIPMENT BEING IN A MAINTAINABLE CONDITION.

PM Programs and Lessons Learned

One thing for sure and the biggest lesson learned is to make sure you have, at the very least, some type of PM program. Without the basics, you will soon be faced with "knee-jerk PMs," which are usually created in the absence of a well-defined and managed PM program.

That said, the second biggest lesson is the managing of the program. So many factors come into play when developing or modifying a program that one tends to forget the management of the program. This is necessary so it doesn't become an untamed beast that is quickly out of control and results in diminishing returns and little to no reliability improvement.

PMs are living documents that require periodic maintenance and tuning, just like the assets for which they were developed. All PMs should be put through an optimization process at least every two years to maintain integrity in your program. One of the best ways to stay on top of this is to actually schedule time and resources to go through the program. In doing so shows a commitment from leadership to continuously improve the workload of its biggest asset, which is the people within the organization.

If a piece of equipment fails, do NOT fall into the trap of "we better get a PM in place for that!" Rather, take the time to understand the equipment and the failure modes associated with it and build a more robust PM program that addresses the elimination of these failure modes. Introduce more predictive routes and use condition monitoring where it makes sense.

Use the tools available that will help you optimize the PMs and go through the existing program. Remove any non-value added tasks, such as single-minute exchange of die (SMED), failure modes analysis, RCM and tribal knowledge.

Preventive maintenance is not truly understood in most organizations around the world. If one would take a minute and think about the results expected from a PM program, things may change. If an organization wants to be physically responsible to its stockholders or owners, then PM must be viewed as an investment and not a cost.

About the Authors

Doug Stangier

Doug Stangier is an electrician by trade and has been in the maintenance field for 20-plus years. He has been in maintenance management and reliability roles for the past 10-plus years. He has a variety of industrial and commercial experience and shares a passion with his coauthor for improving the maintenance reliability processes and the struggles that those who work in the industry face. Doug also holds Certified Maintenance and Reliability Professional (CMRP) and Certified Reliability Leader (CRL) certifications, as well as being a certified Project Manager and Six Sigma Green Belt.

Doug is currently in a maintenance manager role within the forest products industry for Weyerhaeuser at one of its oriented strand board (OSB) manufacturing facilities in Saskatchewan, Canada.

Doug has had the opportunity to work in various mill environments, primarily in the wood products manufacturing industry and has been involved with three CMMS implementations. He was also part of a team that developed a significant road map for maintenance departments within his company called "ToBe" documents, which lay the foundation for planning and scheduling. Doug was a speaker at the 2014 International Maintenance Conference (IMC-2014), where he shared his journey regarding the development of this process, a work management system and the reliability efforts that were part of it.

Having the opportunity to work on this book and being able to share some best practices with fellow maintenance reliability professionals is just another chapter in his career. Having completed this book, Doug is looking forward to doing another one in the near future.

About the Authors

Ricky Smith

Ricky Smith is a Certified Maintenance and Reliability Professional (CMRP) and a certification test proctor, as well as a Certified Maintenance and Reliability Technician (CMRT) certified by the Society for Maintenance and Reliability Professionals (SMRP). He also holds a Certified Plant Maintenance Manager (CPMM) Certification by the Association for Facilities Engineering (AFE) and is a Certified Reliability Leader (CRL) by the Association of Asset Management Professionals (AMP).

Many people and organizations succeed using Ricky Smith's simple approach to any process that creates long-term value. Ricky transitions organizations from their current state to a more proactive state, resulting in culture change, optimal asset reliability and lower costs.

Ricky has over 30 years of experience in manufacturing, facilities, mining, military and many other types of organizations as both a practitioner and change agent in maintenance reliability worldwide. He worked in two corporate roles, one as a global reliability engineering leader and the other as a corporate maintenance engineering leader. At the site level, he began his career as a maintenance technician at Exxon Company USA, Alumax Mt. Holly (this plant was rated the best in the world for over 18 years) and Hercules Chemical, providing the foundation for his maintenance reliability experience.

In 2004, Ricky was mobilized by the U.S. Army Reserve to deploy to Southwest Asia as a Maintenance Company Commander in Operation Iraqi Freedom. He served in this capacity from 2004-2005. In 2007, Ricky was mobilized as the investigating military officer at the Pentagon and charged by Secretary of Defense Robert Gates to identify facility issues and make recommended changes to enhance facility reliability at Walter Reed National Military Medical Center. His report on the facility's condition and problems were reported to the U.S. Congress in 2007. He also wrote an article for *Uptime* Magazine on this issue.

About the Authors

Ricky is the coauthor of "Rules of Thumb for Maintenance and Reliability Engineers," "Lean Maintenance: Reduce Costs, Improve Quality, and Increase Market Share," "Industrial Machinery Repair: Best Maintenance Practices Pocket Guide," "Planning & Scheduling Made Simple," "Maintenance Reliability Metrics/KPIs 101 Keeping It Simple," "Maintenance and Reliability Lubrication 101 Keeping It Simple," "FRACAS, Failure Reporting, Analysis, Corrective Action System" and his newest release, "Root Cause Failure Analysis Made Simple."

Ricky is working on a new book, "How to Optimize a PM Program." He has written for different magazines during the past 25 years on technical, reliability and maintenance subjects.

Ricky is past Chairman of The Society for Maintenance and Reliability Professionals (SMRP) Oil, Gas, and Petrochemicals SIG, which has seven regional directors globally. He is past Chairman of the SMRP's Mining Special Interest Group.

uptime® Elements™
A Reliability Framework for Asset Performance

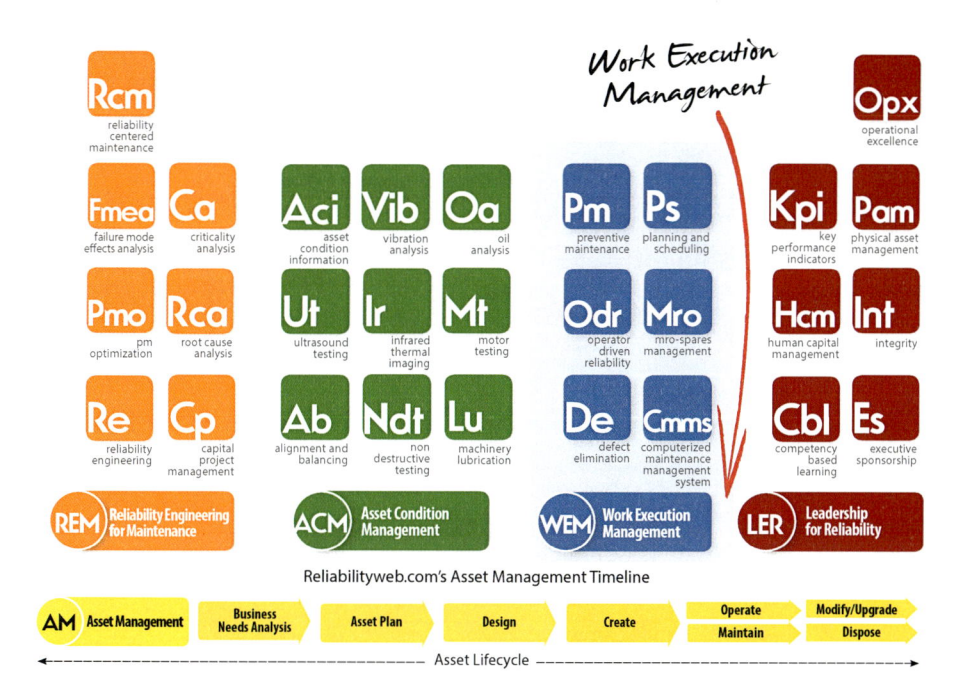

Work Execution Management

Rcm reliability centered maintenance			**Opx** operational excellence
Fmea failure mode effects analysis / **Ca** criticality analysis	**Aci** asset condition information / **Vib** vibration analysis / **Oa** oil analysis	**Pm** preventive maintenance / **Ps** planning and scheduling	**Kpi** key performance indicators / **Pam** physical asset management
Pmo pm optimization / **Rca** root cause analysis	**Ut** ultrasound testing / **Ir** infrared thermal imaging / **Mt** motor testing	**Odr** operator driven reliability / **Mro** mro-spares management	**Hcm** human capital management / **Int** integrity
Re reliability engineering / **Cp** capital project management	**Ab** alignment and balancing / **Ndt** non destructive testing / **Lu** machinery lubrication	**De** defect elimination / **Cmms** computerized maintenance management system	**Cbl** competency based learning / **Es** executive sponsorship
REM Reliability Engineering for Maintenance	**ACM** Asset Condition Management	**WEM** Work Execution Management	**LER** Leadership for Reliability

Reliabilityweb.com's Asset Management Timeline

AM Asset Management → Business Needs Analysis → Asset Plan → Design → Create → Operate / Maintain → Modify/Upgrade / Dispose

------- Asset Lifecycle -------

Uptime Elements are a trademark of Uptime Magazine • ©2012-2014 Reliabilityweb.com • uptimemagazine.com • reliabilityweb.com • maintenance.org

Reliabilityweb.com® and Uptime® Magazine Mission: **To make the people we serve safer and more successful.**
One way we support this mission is to suggest a reliability system for asset performance management as pictured above. Our use of the Uptime Elements is designed to assist you in categorizing and organizing your own Body of Knowledge (BoK) whether it be through training, articles, books or webinars. Our hope is to make YOU safer and more successful.

About Reliabilityweb.com

Created in 1999, Reliabilityweb.com provides educational information and peer-to-peer networking opportunities that enable safe and effective maintenance reliability and asset management for organizations around the world.

Activities Include:

Reliabilityweb.com® (www.reliabilityweb.com) includes educational articles, tips, video presentations, an industry event calendar and industry news. Updates are available through free email subscriptions and RSS feeds. **Confiabilidad.net** is a mirror site that is available in Spanish at www.confiabilidad.net

Uptime® Magazine (www.uptimemagazine.com) is a bi-monthly magazine launched in 2005 that is highly prized by the maintenance reliability and asset management community. Editions are obtainable in both print and digital.

Reliability Leadership Institute® Conferences and Training Events

(www.maintenanceconference.com) offer events that range from unique, focused-training workshops and seminars to small focused conferences to large industry-wide events, including the International Maintenance Conference and The RELIABILITY® Conference.

MRO-Zone Bookstore (www.mro-zone.com) is an online bookstore offering a maintenance reliability and asset management focused library of books, DVDs and CDs published by Reliabilityweb.com.

Association of Asset Management Professionals

(www.maintenance.org) is a member organization and online community that encourages professional development and certification and supports information exchange and learning with 50,000+ members worldwide.

A Word About Social Good

Reliabilityweb.com is mission driven to deliver value and social good to the maintenance reliability and asset management communities. *Doing good work and making profit is not inconsistent*, and as a result of Reliabilityweb.com's mission-driven focus, financial stability and success has been the outcome. For over a decade, Reliabilityweb.com's positive contributions and commitment to the maintenance reliability and asset management communities have been unmatched.

Other Causes

Reliabilityweb.com has financially contributed to include industry associations, such as SMRP, AFE, STLE, ASME and ASTM, and community charities, including the Salvation Army, American Red Cross, Wounded Warrior Project, Paralyzed Veterans of America and the Autism Society of America. In addition, we are proud supporters of our U.S. Troops and first responders who protect our freedoms and way of life. That is only possible by being a for-profit company that pays taxes.

I hope you will get involved with and explore the many resources that are available to you through the Reliabilityweb.com network.

Warmest regards,
Terrence O'Hanlon
CEO, Reliabilityweb.com